LEARNI... ...

BANKING

A GUIDE TO STUDY, REVISION
AND EXAMINATION TECHNIQUES

KEITH ELLIOTT, MA, BA (Econ), FColl P, Cert Ed
Senior Lecturer in Economics, Liverpool Polytechnic

PAUL KELLY, BSc (Econ), ACIB
Manager, International Division, The Royal Bank of Scotland

DON WRIGHT, M Phil, BA (Econ), MIPM
Head of Education & Training, TSB England & Wales

The Chartered Institute of Bankers

First published 1984 by The Institute of Bankers
Reprinted 1985
Reprinted with amendments 1987
Second edition 1988 published by Bankers Books Ltd.
Reprinted 1989

Chartered Institute of Bankers (CIB) Publications are published by Bankers Books Limited under an exclusive license and royalty agreement. Bankers Books Limited is a company owned by The Chartered Institute of Bankers.

Enquiries should be sent to the publishers at the undermentioned address:

BANKERS BOOKS LIMITED
c/o The Chartered Institute of Bankers
10 Lombard Street
London
EC3V 9AS

ISBN 0 85297 216 4

Typeset in 10 on 12pt Times by Commercial Colour Press, London E7 0EW
Text printed on 110 gm² Commercial Cartridge
Printed in the United Kingdom by Commercial Colour Press, London E7 0EW

Contents

1 Studying for a Professional Examination

1—Introduction

You are obviously thinking hard about studying for the Institute's examinations. This booklet is written specifically for you and is designed to help you to understand:

* what the exams are about; how they are organised and the standards expected
* why you should take the exams; how you can study for them and the techniques to apply to pass them
* the discipline required
* the time needed and how to use it

2—The Institute's examinations

The idea behind the examinations is that they are based on a course of study that helps staff in banking institutions:

* to acquire a sound knowledge of such basic commercial topics as economics, law, and accountancy, and how they apply to banking
* to learn about specific aspects of banking practice (or the skills of executor and trusteeship), which will help them in their work and in making progress to senior positions

Passing the associateship examinations demonstrates that you have *successfully* completed a very demanding course of study. The award of the ACIB is proof that you hold a valuable and well-respected professional qualification.

The curriculum

The ACIB examination is divided into two main parts.

Stage 1 is the stage which all students (except graduates of a recognised institution) must take to allow them to proceed to Stage 2.

Stage 1 can be completed in two main ways.

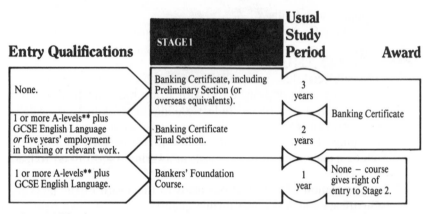

Entry Qualifications — **STAGE 1** — **Usual Study Period** — **Award**

Entry Qualifications	STAGE 1	Usual Study Period	Award
None.	Banking Certificate, including Preliminary Section (or overseas equivalents).	3 years	Banking Certificate
1 or more A-levels** plus GCSE English Language *or* five years' employment in banking or relevant work.	Banking Certificate Final Section.	2 years	
1 or more A-levels** plus GCSE English Language.	Bankers' Foundation Course.	1 year	None – course gives right of entry to Stage 2.

**Or two AS levels.

(a) *Banking Certificate*

This course is in two parts.

In the Preliminary Section, usually studied over a year, you will be polishing the basic skills of business life as they are used in banking. The subjects covered are:

> Business Calculations
> Business Communications
> The Business of Banking

If you obtain at least 65% in all three papers, you may, if you wish, enter the Foundation Course if you intend to enter for the Banking Diploma.

In the Final Section of six subjects you will be looking more closely into the areas of national life that affect banks directly and indirectly through changes in the fortunes, opportunities and constraints experienced both by banks and their customers.

This group of subjects is:

Economics and the Banks' Role in the Economy
Introduction to Accounting
Banking: The Legal Environment

Other subjects introduce you to the problems of running a bank and dealing with customers. Here you will study:

Supervisory Skills
Banking Operations 1—International Business & Lending
Banking Operations 2—Customer Service & Marketing

The subjects that you will be studying are very relevant and interesting and will provide you with a firm base on which to build your career. A benefit for students taking the Banking Certificate is that you can take as many subjects a year as you feel capable of handling. Experience would suggest that for Stage 2 students, taking a maximum of two subjects at a sitting is most likely to lead to success.

Completion of both sections leads to the award of the Banking Certificate which is a worthwhile qualification in its own right.

The examination will also prove to be a good grounding for those students who want to progress to Stage 2 and gain the Banking Diploma.

(b) *Foundation Course*
This approach to the Stage 2 examinations may be preferred by those with at least one A-level plus a GCSE in English Language (or equivalents). If your A-levels are not in subjects related to banking, you may find the Foundation Course hard going.

It is better, therefore, to study for the Banking Certificate which not only gives a recognised qualification but provides a thorough grounding in the subjects to be studied in Stage 2.

If, however, you are confident enough to study for the Foundation Course, you work will cover:

Economics
Structure of Accounts
General Principles of Law
Elements of Banking
   or
Elements of Investment

3

Passing the Foundation Course does not lead to any qualifications; it enables you to enter the Stage 2 examinations.

Stage 2—The Institute's Diploma examinations

The Institute now has three different Stage 2 examinations leading to the award of the ACIB:

The Banking Diploma
The Trustee Diploma
The International Banking Diploma

Whichever you opt for in the light of your work in the bank, or your career prospects, Stage 2 will give you a good background in applied business studies, a basic knowledge of banking practice (or executor and trustee work) together with an introduction to management.

Details of subjects and regulations for these examinations are published in separate syllabuses which are available to members free of charge.

Although you can sit as many subjects as you like during the Institute's exams in May and October, you should be realistic. Normally two subjects are the maximum that should be attempted at any one sitting.

The standards required

You should appreciate that the Institute's examinations are not, and are not meant to be, easy. They are a test in both quantity and depth of material. They should, therefore, only be taken by students who are willing to study effectively and devote sufficient time and effort to their work.

As a generalisation, the Stage 2 examination is equivalent to a degree qualification, which gives you an idea of the standards required.

3—Motivation

From what has been said you will see that getting your ACIB will take anything from three to six years. To study over such a long period will take a lot of effort but it will in the long run be worthwhile. Qualifying as an ACIB:

* shows your commitment to your career and your bank
* demonstrates your ability to understand the key areas of banking
* illustrates your professionalism
* points to your desire to progress to a management role

This final point is important, for in many banks failure to qualify as an ACIB may be a serious obstacle in progression to becoming a manager.

Working for the exams is a way of increasing your skill and knowledge and it helps you to get better at your job. This is surely one of the key motivations behind your studies.

4—The difference from being at school

There are several major differences between studying for GCSE and 'A' levels, and studying for a professional exam.

(a) *When you study*
You have to combine a full day's work with your study programme. This means that you have to fit most of your studying into evenings and weekends, even if you are fortunate enough to have day release from your bank. This may mean you have to study when you don't feel like it or when you would rather be out with your friends.

(b) *Pressure on your time*
You will find lots of things to do with your time; playing a sport, listening to records, going to the cinema and so on. In fact you could easily fill all your time with non-study activity.

If you are going to pass you will have to make time for your studies. This means you will have to plan your time carefully, if you are to fit in your social and study activity.

(c) *Planning for yourself*
At school your teachers probably planned your work for you. All you had to do was learn the material and do your homework. Now you are studying for a professional exam you are left more on your own. You have to plan:

5

* what you are going to study
* how to study it
* when to work
* when and whether to complete your homework

(d) *Exams are work related*

On the brighter side, the material you will be studying is often related to your job and should therefore be more interesting than some of your school subjects. Not only can you start to apply some of your 'learning' to your job; the work you do in the branch can also help you with your studies.

(e) *Studying is not cramming*

Some students think that they will pass by learning parrot-fashion, by cramming facts, and then regurgitating them all over the exam paper. Studying for the ACIB is more interesting than this. It is about understanding your studies (and your work) and about applying your knowledge to a variety of banking situations.

(f) *Being professional*

You work in a demanding and 'professional' organisation, where you are expected to do your job to the best of your ability. You should apply the same standards to your studying. Remember no one is going to keep checking on how much study work you are doing, and ask to see your homework.

No one is going to give you 'lines' or detention! It is left in most cases to your own dedication and professionalism to ensure that you study regularly and effectively throughout the year. If you do, you will have very little trouble with the exams.

2 Preparing to Study

Before you read about some of the study techniques you can use, there are a few important areas of which you should be aware.

1—Keeping up-to-date

The banking world today is one of continuous and rapid change. This means of course that you will need to keep up-to-date with new material that affects your exams.

There are several ways you can guarantee being up-to-date. These are:

(a) *Course syllabus*
A copy of the course syllabus is an essential document for all serious students. You need to know what topics are to be studied in order that you can:

   * plan your work
   * cover the essentials of the subject.

The Institute issues to students who are elected to membership a booklet containing the regulations, syllabus and recommended reading relating to your course of study. This is not for filing: it is for *reading and studying* so that you will know what is expected of you.

Remember that syllabuses change, so make sure you are always working on the latest one.

(b) *Examiners' Reports*
The Institute publishes Examiners' Reports for the Stage 1 and Stage 2 Spring and Autumn exams. These reports are a *must*. They contain:

   * guidelines to the answer
   * notes of common mistakes

* hints about techniques
* up-to-date study information
* the exam papers

Studying these reports should be a key activity throughout the year, although they are particularly useful at year end revision.

(c) *Banking World*

Members of the Institute receive copies of the journal *Banking World*. This publication contains articles on current banking matters, information about changes in both banking practice and the examinations, and even contains model answers to past questions.

This journal is essential reading for all ACIB students. Examiners expect you to read it and often look for information from the journal to be included in your exam answers.

(d) *Stage 1 Bulletin*

This provides students studying for the Banking Certificate and Foundation Course up-to-date information on the syllabus together with hints and advice from Chief Examiners and tutors. The Stage 1 Bulletin is available in Spring and Autumn.

(e) *General reading*

Banking and the banking exams are about the 'living' world and you should therefore keep up-to-date with what is going on. You can do this by reading a quality daily and Sunday paper and some of the many journals and magazines that relate to your business, e.g. *The Economist*. This wider reading helps you to understand the financial scene and the business of banking and this in turn will help you to pass your exams.

2—How you should study

We have already mentioned that you are now a part-time student who has to combine a 'day' job with a study programme.

In order to study in the way that suits you best, you should give some thought to the options available.

(a) *Colleges*

There are colleges throughout the country where you can get oral tuition for both Stage 1 and Stage 2 courses. Some courses are held during the day, for day-release students, although most colleges also provide evening classes for other ACIB students.

Many students like to go to college because this offers:

* regularity and discipline
* contact with a tutor
* someone to answer questions
* a series of homework for marking and comment
* contact with a group of students studying the same subject

To get the best out of college you should:

* go regularly even when it is cold and wet, or there's something on TV you would like to see
* participate in class, ask questions and have discussions, *don't just copy out notes*
* complete homework on time
* not rely solely on your teacher to get you through
* work at times other than during your college attendance

(b) *Correspondence courses*

There are several correspondence colleges which provide tuition for both stages of the Institute's examinations. The written material supplied by these colleges is usually self-contained so that you won't need to buy recommended textbooks. On these courses you work at home studying the material sent by the college.

These courses are popular with students because they provide:

* flexibility—you can study at any convenient time and are not tied to one or two evenings a week
* a regular contact with tutors, by post, usually through marked homework
* a study programme to meet your needs
* a conditional guarantee of teaching until you pass the exam
* material that is regularly updated

9

They do however demand:

* self-discipline
* working on your own without regular contact with a class of students

(c) *Private study*

It is possible to study, on your own, for the exams using either recommended books or some of the study packs that are available. This option is not open to Stage 1 Foundation students who have to study with an approved college.

The advantage of this method is that you can work at your own pace in your own time.

To be successful, however, you will need to:

* have enough self-discipline to do the work needed
* work without tutor guidance
* contact other students yourself
* get your written work marked by other students or even mark it yourself

Private study is very hard work and we would not really recommend it except perhaps for a re-sit exam.

3—You and studying

You may have got the impression that the ACIB exams are not a 'doddle'. You are right, but that does not mean they are too difficult for you to take and pass.

To be a successful student three things are essential:

* basic ability
* consistent work
* study technique

(a) *Ability*

It is probably true to say that very few Institute students lack the ability to pass. Bank staff are intelligent people who have already achieved success at school.

Students do not fail the exam because they are stupid; they fail because of a lack of consistent effort and ineffective study technique.

(b) *Consistent work*

The courses you will be studying will require you to work steadily over a period of months. You will have little chance of passing if you try a quick two-month cramming job.

The secret of success is to work consistently each week throughout your study year, avoiding the temptation to take a week off or even miss one of your evening sessions.

The student who works regularly greatly improves his or her chance of passing. This is not as easy as it sounds. You will be pressurised by friends and relations to come out for a drink, or have a night off. You will need the courage to say 'sorry not tonight—I'm studying'.

You will also need courage to deal with yourself. You are going to have to:

* take a demanding exam where failure is always a possibility
* organise your lifestyle to include studying as an important part
* aim for success rather than take the easy way out by not trying

As well as needing courage you are going to have to think positively. Let's face it, there will be times when you will get discouraged:

* you have a cold
* you can't grasp a point
* your homework is marked down

One thing you must avoid is the downward spiral of negative thought. Once you start thinking you can't do it, you will soon find ways of proving this.

Be positive: you already have a record of achievement, you can, and you will, pass. Keep telling yourself—'you're good'.

(c) *Study technique*

The rest of this booklet describes some of the study techniques you can use to help you pass the exam. Before you can apply these however, you will need to create study time.

11

4—Creating the time

(a) *Where to get the time*

Lack of time is the most common excuse given by students for failing their exams. Mind you they did have time for watching TV, playing football twice a week, going to keep-fit classes, and so on. What they are really saying is that they preferred to use their time to do other things.

The first thing you have got to do is make time every week for your studies. Work out what you are going to give up to fit your study in; set aside the time in the evenings or at weekends and then stick to it.

Study regularly at the same times each week. It helps you, your friends and relations to get into a routine.

(b) *What to do with it*

The objective of any studying is to get to the exam having covered the subjects detailed in the course syllabus. To help you do this you should prepare an overall outline plan for the whole year which shows what you are going to cover and by what date.

You should then produce a timetable each week which details the topics you should cover in each of your study sessions.

(c) *Avoiding its disappearance*

Given half a chance, time will 'disappear'. Three hours can easily be wasted with a couple of daydreams, three cups of coffee, a telephone call, and forty winks. You must discipline yourself to avoid time wasting. You can do this by:

* knowing what you are going to study when you sit down
* avoiding distractions
* working in short bursts, say 45 minutes, then taking a 5 to 10 minute break
* studying in the same room each time

However, the key discipline you need is regularity. Remember the more often you do something the better you become at it. The same applies to studying.

(d) *Using the half hours*

Many students think that they need 2 or 3 hours to do any useful studying and, therefore, ignore a valuable source of time. Half hours are easy to find (and waste). Look how you spend your time and you will see that you can generate many half hours in a week, e.g. at lunch times, travelling to work on a bus or train. Because they are quite short periods you will need to think what you are going to use them for. Do not just pick up a book and read for half an hour; you need to apply the advice given on page 14 to your half-hour periods.

What do you do in half-hour periods? You could:

* write an exam answer
* plan an answer to an essay
* learn a definition
* mark an exam answer
* make notes on an examiner's report

(e) *Do's and don'ts of weekly study*

   (i) *Do*
       * Ensure that you discuss your timetable with your girl/boy-friend or husband/wife to ensure domestic support and agreement;
       * get into a routine—soon your friends will get to know that you are not available at particular times in the week;
       * build in some flexibility to top up any shortfall in your allocated study periods;
       * build in some leisure activity preferably as much 'fresh air' as possible;
       * avoid gaps of days between study periods—regularity keeps the momentum going and makes for more effective learning;
       * work in short bursts of about 45 minutes before stretching the legs and having a drink. It keeps the circulation going, prevents staleness, and you will return after a 5 to 10 minute break refreshed.

   (ii) *Don't*
       * Plan to work for longer than three hours without a long break. Long continuous periods of 'swotting' tend to lead to

13

loss of concentration, bad temper, and a reduction in guilt rather than ignorance;

* normally plan to cover in a single day not more than two 3-hour or three 2-hour study periods;
* burn the midnight oil—working into the early hours produces yawns not effective learning;
* leave study work over to the 'next week'—if need be, create more time now;
* concentrate solely on completing 'homework'.

3 Learning Effectively

1—The basis of effective learning

(a) *The three levels of learning*

It is very important as a first step in improving your learning efficiency to appreciate the three levels of learning.

Level one consists of the facts or the details; *level two* of the links and interrelations between those facts, and *level three*, the overall theories or analytical structures that claim to make sense of these interrelated facts.

Facts alone tell you little or nothing. The annual rate of inflation may be 5%, but so what? The *level one* fact does not tell you that inflation is rising or falling, or is higher or lower than in other countries. So you need to look for other interrelated facts, at *level two*, to give it real meaning. However, even when you have these you still need to consider, at *level three*, the alternative theories regarding the causes of inflation before you fully understand the topic.

You will notice that, as you climb the 'educational ladder', less emphasis is placed on memorising facts and more on the higher levels of learning.

(b) *The three key principles*

You will learn most if you are up to PAR. This brief mnemonic stands for:

Purpose
Activity
Recall

Purpose

You tend to learn most when you have a clear purpose and objective in mind, knowing what you want to achieve and having determination to achieve it.

Activity

So often students passively read books or re-read old notes, and not surprisingly the eyes get glued to one line while the mind wanders to last night's TV or weekend's disco. Such lapses of concentration can be prevented by introducing activity methods of learning, as explained later.

Recall

You will build your learning most effectively if you really secure your understanding at each stage as you build up your knowledge. It is very important to 'know that you know' by recalling and placing in your memory bank each deposit of learning as you go.

These PAR principles are behind all the advice in the remaining chapters so let's start to use them.

2—Getting the most from a study period

(a) *Set targets*

Remember Christopher Columbus? Cynics have observed that when he set out he did not know where he was going; when he arrived he did not know where he was, and when he came back he did not know where he had been!

So at the start of each study period:

* Set a clear target of what you want to achieve
* Gear your target to the time available

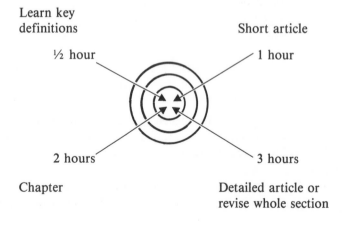

Learn key definitions

Short article

½ hour

1 hour

2 hours

3 hours

Chapter

Detailed article or revise whole section

(b) *Be active*

Try to introduce as much activity as possible as this will make your learning both more effective and more enjoyable. Avoid just sitting passively reading. Try:

* talking to yourself repeating key points
* making concise accurate notes
* writing a brief summary of key points
* building up a card index of key definitions

(c) *Test yourself*

When?

At the end of every study period it is very important that you test yourself to find out if you can recall what you have learnt to see if you have hit your target.

Why?

You should do this check-out because:

* revision should not be a 'rushed' activity at the end of the year but a continuous checking-out process
* it creates activity and reinforces the learning target set for the study period
* memory fades so it is crucial to cement understanding straightaway
* it builds confidence as you prove to yourself that you really recalled the material
* understanding fresh material is easier because old material was 'checked out'. Your memory is like a rolling snowball which expands by continuous reinforcement of old material and the addition of new.

How?

With notes hidden and books shut use some of these check-out methods:

* take a blank piece of paper and create a new form of note
* answer a past exam question in a time-constrained mock exam
* complete a short summary
* talk to yourself speaking an 'oral essay' of the key points; tape it and play it back

3—Reading to some purpose

(a) *Map out the material first*

As time is scarce and much of your reading will be of recommended texts try not to just dive straight into reading Chapter One. Before you start to read specific chapters it is worthwhile to survey, or map out, the book as a whole.

So before dipping into the chapters themselves it is worthwhile to skim:

* the title page
* the preface
* the table of contents
* the index

After you have done that, flick through from the front, not the back, of the book to:

* note the main sections and chapter headings
* check if there are summaries at the end of chapters
* look at any visuals such as charts, graphs or tables
* read and sample a few sentences

Now, if you are to read an article, or a single chapter, flick through looking particularly for:

* any foreword
* the opening paragraph which may give the author's own survey of what is to come
* subheadings showing you the route to be taken
* any italics showing key concepts or vital areas
* the final paragraph or conclusion which may summarise the essence of what has been said

(b) *Create questions before you read*

Before you read, a really valuable skill is to create questions, the answers to which you expect are in the article or chapter. It is a *really vital* exercise because:

* by creating the questions you will bring to the forefront of your mind your existing knowledge—this is a form of mental 'warm-up'

* new material is more likely to be retained as it can be linked to your existing knowledge
* your concentration will improve as you look for the answers to your questions.

So prior to reading, create questions:

* for each of the three levels of learning
* using what, why, where, when, who and how as your guides

Let us see how this might work. Imagine you are going to read an article on 'The Bank of England and Monetary Policy'. You might generate the following questions prior to reading it:

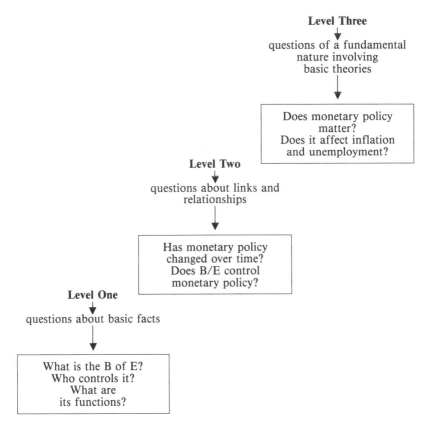

Level Three

questions of a fundamental
nature involving
basic theories

Does monetary policy
matter?
Does it affect inflation
and unemployment?

Level Two

questions about links and
relationships

Has monetary policy
changed over time?
Does B/E control
monetary policy?

Level One

questions about basic facts

What is the B of E?
Who controls it?
What are
its functions?

Doing this will:

* bring to the forefront of your mind your existing knowledge to which the new material you read will be linked
* give your reading a greater purpose as you look for the answers to your questions
* re-emphasise the importance of the three levels of learning

(c) *Notemaking when reading*

Why?
Whenever you read you should make notes because:
* this creates activity and aids concentration
* it provides a written record which can provide raw material both for essays, and later examination preparation and revision
* without notes you rely on memory which tends to fade over time

First reading—no notes
We recommend on first reading you should look for:
* the higher levels of learning
* the main ideas and key points
* the relationship between them

We do not think you should make any notes until a second reading.

Why wait?
The reason for this is that if you make notes on your first reading:
* you do not yet know what the main points are or the overall thread of the argument
* you will therefore concentrate on detail rather than see the whole picture
* you will tend to forget your questions
* it will distract you and slow you down
* you will tend to copy words from the book rather than use your own expressions so that when the notes are later used for essays you can be accused of repeating things 'parrot-fashion'
* you will make more notes than you need.

4—Making notes

(a) *Be 'easy on the eye'*

Effective notes are concise and accurate records of main ideas, key points, and relationships. To be effective they must remain easy to read and understand in the future when they come to be used. The test to apply now is simple ... Will I understand them in months to come? The secret of effective note-making is therefore not to make notes that are grammatically correct pieces of flowing prose, similar to pieces of essay writing. Note-making is a different skill where you must be brief and *easy on the eye*, and to achieve this you can use:

The SACHA Guidelines
  S*paces*
  A*bbreviations*
  C*olour*
  H*eadings*
  A*rtistic devices*

(i) *Spaces*

The reasons for creating space is purely practical. It allows you to:

* read notes more easily
* find specific points
* add to the notes at a later date—notes need space so do not squash them up
* leave 1½″ as a margin
* write on every other line

(ii) *Abbreviations*

Using abbreviations as a form of shorthand helps you to:

* maintain the thread of your second reading avoiding long breaks while you write
* keep up with the lecturer
* develop an abbreviation system which will remain of value long after you have passed your exams

Abbreviations speed up note-making so:
* develop your own system and stick with it

There are six main types of abbreviations:

First part of word only	First part and last letter	Initials	Figures	Useful symbols	Standard abbreviations
org.	bk.	c.i.f.	C19th	>	e.g.
agric.	decln.	E.E.C.	£10bn.	=	viz.
incl.	dept.	N.B.	½	↑	etc.

* do not chop and change them
* practise using them regularly

(iii) *Colours*

The use of colour helps to avoid the boredom of reading page after page of biro notes but perhaps more importantly it:

* lends vitality and attraction
* highlights key points
* draws the eye to certain sections

(iv) *Headings*

The use of headings, either in capital letters or by underlining is important to:

* tell you the key areas
* provide the overall picture
* act as a memory jogger
* show secondary points by using sub-headings

(v) *Artistic devices*

The main devices you use are:

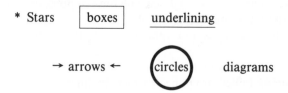

22

By using these you can:

* create space, encourage creation of headings, and develop use of colour
* highlight main points
* break up dull prose
* show movement and relationships

(b) *Vertical notes*
This is the traditional method of note-making with notes written:

* from the top of the page to the bottom
* along lines from left to right
* usually on ruled paper—this form of note-making is useful but it is not the only kind of note you can make

(c) *Horizontal space notes*
Here note-making takes on a different shape and format as:

* you use the page sideways to create width
* you break the tyranny of the ruled lines

There are three main forms of horizontal space notes:

* the patterned note
* the flow diagram and
* the horizontal frame

(i) *The patterned note*
In this method you work out from a central key point towards the edges of the paper by:

* selecting a phrase or word describing the key point and placing this at the centre of the page
* adding the main facts and joining these to the centre point by lines
* adding to the main facts in similar fashion
* then joining linked or connected facts by lines

The way in which such a pattern can develop is shown below. It is a method that we find increasingly used by students, so if you have not used it very often before, give it a go. It has a number of advantages, namely:

* the main point is clearly identified
* the relative importance of items is shown by the nearness to the centre
* links between the points are easily recognisable
* new points can easily be added
* quick and effective recall is produced as the pattern shape aids memory

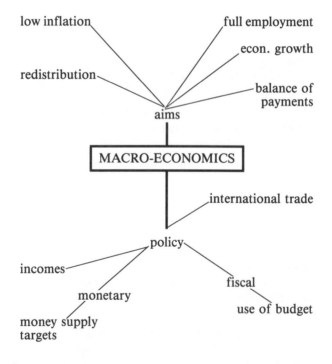

(ii) *The flow diagram*
Flow diagrams can often be used as many points are linked together.

They are especially useful when:

* points flow from one to another
* there is a clear sequence of events
* time or processes are involved

Just look at and study the following flow diagram of *The monetarist view of the cause of inflation.*

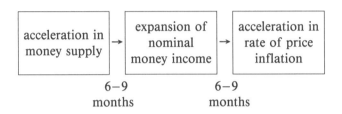

6−9
months

6−9
months

whole cycle takes
12−18 months

You will find that after studying it for only 30−60 seconds you can remember it and reproduce it quite accurately. This shows that valuable visually attractive notes are also notes you will remember.

(iii) *Horizontal frames*
Notes here are made in column form across the page. You place:

* the headings across the top of the page
* the areas of comparison or contrast vertically
* the 'key point' notes below the appropriate heading

The advantages of this method are that it:

* lets you see possible linkages across key areas
* helps you to compare and contrast data
* is valuable during revision in preparation for 'compare and contrast' questions in the exam

In the following horizontal frame you look across the five vertical headings to compare and contrast the essential features of a partnership and a limited company.

Item	Partnership	Company
1. Liability of members	Unlimited	Limited
2. Membership	Not over 20 (with certain exceptions)	Normally no maximum
3. Management	By partners, who all have right to take part in management	Delegated by shareholders to directors
4. Regulations	Contained in formal or informal (sometimes unwritten) agreement	Defined in the stamped and registered Memorandum and Articles
5. Main legislation	Loose control by Partnership Act 1890, and Limited Partnerships Act 1907	Close control by modern Companies Acts
6. Capital	Easily varied. It fluctuates, since profits, drawings, etc. are often adjusted in capital accounts	Fixed by Memorandum. Strict regulations on variations
7. Status	No identity separate from partners	Separate legal entity—a corporate 'person'

Use of horizontal space notes

(a) *For check at the end of a study period:*
Put away your other notes and books now and see if you can create a fresh horizontal note. The process of creating it will reinforce your memory.

(b) *Copying notes*
Instead of neatly rewriting notes made at college try converting them from a vertical to a horizontal format. The process of conversion will be a valuable learning experience.

4 Revision Strategy

1—Revision—an all year round activity

Many students believe that revision is an activity that is confined to a very short period immediately before the exam, and consists of cramming information in the hope that it can be reproduced on the day. This is a poor approach. Successful revision is an all year round activity that should involve a planned build-up of knowledge.

So remember to:

* check out at the end of each study period to ensure that 'you know you know'
* use the last week of each term to revise that term's work concentrating on the key areas of study
* 'Copy' your class notes not just by rewriting them but by creating a fresh horizontal space note. By turning our original notes into a different format you will have a learning experience not just a handwriting experience!

By revising in these ways and by practising the points made in the last chapter you will enter the pre-exam revision period well prepared.

2—Pre-exam revision

Students sometimes spend only a week or so in final pre-exam revision when ideally it would be best to have eight weeks or so. However, it is probably unrealistic to expect you to have completed your courses with so much time left, desirable though that would be.

Therefore, a realistic pre-exam revision period should probably cover at least, say, four to six weeks.

(a) *Creating an overall revision plan*

To get the best from your period of pre-exam revision you should create an overall plan. This plan will include:

* an overall routine timetable of topics and subjects to be covered, in sequence, for the whole of the revision period
* a detailed weekly timetable, constructed probably each weekend, allocating specific topics to specific 'time slots'.

The reasons for creating such a plan are that it:

* provides a clear, structured framework
* ensures necessary work is completed on time
* ensures all appropriate work is revised
* provides the security of a professional approach
* gives weekly 'before and after' benefits

The week in prospect:

* provides clear framework
* allocates time efficiently
* sets a weekly target
* reduces anxiety

The week in retrospect:

* allows achievement to be seen
* provides reassurance
* reinforces positive approach
* negative thoughts fade

When creating the plan remember the principles of good 'time-tabling', some of which we examined in Chapter 2.

* Get into a routine—this helps you, your friends and your family
* Use the same 'time slots' each week

* Avoid gaps of days between study periods
* Short 30 minute slots can be used effectively
* Build in some flexibility for leisure
* Discuss your timetable with your spouse, boyfriend or girlfriend so that they know what you are doing and can give you support and agreement.

(b) *Length of each study period*

It is worth remembering that long periods of 'swotting' well into the early morning tend to reduce guilt rather than increase knowledge. The best advice is to:

* work in short bursts (45 – 60 minutes) before a short break and a cup of tea or coffee
* create 30 minute revision sessions. It is surprising how many can be found and how useful they can be
* study for no more than about 3 hours at a stretch before a long break of at least an hour.

3—Revision sources

To create your overall revision plan you will need copies of:

* the exam timetable
* as many past papers as possible
* examiners' reports
* specimen or model answers when available
* the up-to-date course syllabus

You should try to get the 'feel' of each paper you are to take so that you know and understand the nature and structure of the examination itself.

Past papers can help you to answer a number of key questions:

* how long is the exam?
* how many questions are on the paper?

* are there any sections within it?
* do all question carry equal marks?
* is there a compulsory question?
* do certain subjects appear regularly'
* how many questions must I answer?

Examiners' Report can provide the answers to other questions:

* what are the main errors to avoid?
* to what depth should you answer a question?
* what particular points does the examiner expect?
* how is the paper marked?

There are *four* other questions to answer.

1 *Should you revise all the syllabus?*
If the exam provides for choice—No. You can omit less important areas not subject to any compulsory question. However, always select sufficient topics to provide adequate 'insurance' cover.

2 *What are the crucial areas you must revise?*
Those that cover the foundations of the subject such as the essentials of economic theory and topics such as negotiability in the 'Law Relating to Banking' paper that are likely to form part of any compulsory question.

3 *What is the best sequence for revision?*
Start with the crucial areas that you must revise, as many other areas depend on them.

4 *Should you spend less time on subjects you like least?*
No—this is negative. Try to balance your time equally among all subjects.

4—How not to revise

You will recall from Chapter 3 that *activity* is one of the principles of effective learning. The trouble is that so many students are passive. Well, ... has this ever happened to you?

You sit rereading old notes until fairly soon the mind wanders. You know what we mean ... the eyes are transfixed on one line while the mind switches to fantasies about summer holidays or last week's disco. Suddenly you shake your head wondering why you have lost concentration. Then you blame yourself.

'I'll never pass anyway'
'This is boring'

These negative thoughts flood in and you decide as a result to:

* give up and put yourself out of your misery
* introduce new material not studied before in an effort to break the boredom
* concentrate on the course, or syllabus section you enjoy most in an effort to introduce some enjoyment to your revision

So if you want to revise *ineffectively:*

* just passively reread old notes
* do not give yourself targets
* never test yourself

5—Effective revision

By contrast, for revision to be effective you should remember the principles of purpose, activity and recall, so at the start of every revision session have a clear idea of what you want to learn by its end.

To enable you to learn more effectively and to test your understanding *seven* activity methods can be used.

(a) *Creation of fresh notes*
Notes are a key revision source, but as has already been stated, just rereading them is an ineffective method of learning and remembering.

A more effective method is to be active and create new notes in new ways in a more concise form using your existing notes as a basis.

* If your notes are in a traditional vertical form convert them into a horizontal space note.
* Remember the value of horizontal frames for revision involving comparisons and contrasts between two policies, institutions or theories.
* Rewriting existing notes is not as effective as putting their content in a new note format.

This approach will:

* make learning easier
* force conciseness and concentration on key points and the links between them
* aid memory
* create interest and activity

(b) *Card index system*
Several institutions are now producing cards of postcard size, for use in revision. These cards are a second best alternative to producing your own card system.
For each topic it is useful to create a card containing:

* definitions
* major examples
* key authors/names/dates
* four or five key points

These cards are very useful in the days before the exam when you want:

* wide coverage
* speedy revision
* easy access
* last minute reassurance

(c) *Talking to yourself*
Although this sounds rather odd it can be a valuable method of revision.
You can use it to:

* test your grasp of a section of work
* test the achievement of your target

* cement understanding
* introduce variety amongst other methods

Use tape feedback:

* Record your 'talking to yourself'. This is very useful to allow the spotting of errors or omissions.
* You can use your own 'tapes' in your personal stereo as you take the dog for a walk or go for a jog. You will be surprised how much will stick, as repetition aids memory.

(d) *Create fresh exam questions*
One of the great mistakes that you can make is to be too fully prepared for the exam papers of the last five year. You will be able to answer those questions because they have become familiar, almost like old friends, but then, when this year's exam comes you may find:

* the questions are new and phrased differently
* the unfamiliar paper is a 'shock'
* you have become a bit flexible in using your knowledge as it is geared to past questions. The way to avoid this danger is not to avoid past questions. They form part of the professional student's approach. The secret is to role-play the examiner.

Create new questions:

* on your own
* with fellow students in your branch or bank
* on topics likely to come up; but phrase them differently
* with an emphasis on any recent developments in course content, e.g. changes in the law relating to finance
* in the form of a fresh up to date paper

If you do this you will find the 'newness' of the exam will not come too much as a surprise as you will already have 'put yourself in the position of the examiner'.

(e) *Writing examination answers*
Surprisingly most students spend their revision time solely in reading activity, as a preparation for a written exam.

A professional preparation for a written exam must involve writing under exam conditions.

In some of your revision periods you should write answers to past or freshly created exam questions ensuring that you:

* keep to the time you will have in the exam
* do not use books, or notes
* are not distracted by telephones, TV etc.

There are three alternative forms this activity can take:

(i) *Single answer.* This method should be used early in your revision programme and you should know the topic of the question in advance. You could build in some element of surprise by producing several questions on the topic and selecting one at random.

(ii) *Two questions in a row.* This builds up your technique and here you can either know the topics for the questions in advance or produce questions on a variety of topics and select at random.

(iii) *A whole paper.* This would come later in your revision programme. You could use a specific single exam paper or select and amalgamate questions from several papers.

(f) *Marking exam answers*
The very act of marking your own answers or those created with other students is a useful revision activity.

Do this:

* in a 'swop shop' session with others
* on your own at least a day after you have written the answers when they are 'cold'.

You can then analyse them for:

* structure
* relevance
* definitions
* key points included or omitted

Do remember that:

* you should not be worried by small omissions or minor errors in your answers
* you should concentrate on the strengths of the answers
* you will be surprised and reassured to discover just how much you know

(g) *Examiners' reports as a basis for note-making*
For each set of exams at Stage 2 the Institute publishes a booklet of Question Papers and Examiners' Reports. As we stressed in the early pages of Chapter 2 copies of recent reports are a *must* for the professional student. The examiners' reports are a mine of information. They are an ideal basis for active revision.

So:
* create revision cards on key topics using patterned notes
* create fresh notes on model answers
* supplement existing notes

6—Improving your memory

By following the three principles of effective learning and the detailed ways by which you can apply them you will improve your memory.

Nevertheless, although as we have stressed the Institute's examinations are not just about rote memorisation of facts, it is useful when revising to use a few memory techniques based on the way memory works.

How memory works
Your memory is like a series of huge spiders' webs laid on top of each other and all linked together. It contains a vast 'bank' of information.

To use your memory you need two things:

(i) Positive thinking. A real belief that you can remember anything you choose.

(ii) The ability to store information in your spider's web and to recall information from it using the principle of *links*.

To make coursework memorable you need to create links or associations, preferably absurd, silly or even ringing, to enable you to easily recall parts of the syllabus.

Mnemonics as a memory aid

This popular technique involves bringing together the initial letters of some key facts to form a word. The mnemonic acts as the link to trigger the associations and so to ease the process of recall.

Two useful mnemonics connected with bank lending illustrate the point:

	Character
Purpose	Ability
Amount	Management
Repayment	Profitability
Term	Acceptability
Security	Repayment
	Insurance (Sec.)

You can create these for yourself when revising and possibly write them on to your revision cards.

Remembering the number

Statistics are important in the exams to illustrate points and to lend weight and substance to your answer. If you wish to remember numbers or figures here are some useful tips.

Are numbers linked?

Sometimes the same digits occur in numbers that need to be recalled. For example the Bank of England opened in 1694 and was nationalised in 1946. Notice anything about the dates? The digits are the same but in a different order. A valuable aid to remembering them.

Can the number be turned into times?

Often digits occur in a way that enables you to turn them into times. For example 13,401,450 can be remembered as the 13.40 train leaving before the 14.50.

Do the statistics add up?

2,228 can be remembered as its separate parts 22 and 28 sum to 50. So remember half a century and perhaps then create an association, possibly a cricketing one.

However, memory techniques like these are only an aid and should be seen as part of the overall package of principles and practices recommended for you to use when learning and revising in the build up to the examination.

The memory bank
Remember you memory is *not* like a bin in which more can only be added if some material is thrown away. It is more like a bank—but a special bank. Imagine it's advertisement

JOIN THE MEMORY BANK

* Open every weekend
* Rising interest guaranteed
* Never 'in the red'
* Withdrawals without notice

BUILD UP YOUR ACCOUNT TODAY

5 The Examination

1—Before the exam

(a) *During the last few days*

* Revise the revision which has been taking place throughout your study, concentrating on relationships between points
* Use the period to remember such items as definitions, accounting ratios, legal cases, which may be used to illustrate answers
* Avoid overemphasis on the first paper where more than one exam is to be taken

(b) *On the evening before*

* Try to get some fresh air and exercise
* Avoid exhausting yourself by last minute revision until the early hours—you are unlikely to perform well with a weary body and a jaded mind

(c) *On the day of the examination*
Ensure that you have made the necessary practical arrangements.

* Make sure you know when and where the exam is taking place
* Check that you have the correct equipment—pens, pencils, ruler, fluorescent marker pen, and calculator (with new batteries)
* Adopt a positive attitude—you are about to seize an opportunity for which you are well prepared.

2—The exam

Coping with tension
Most of us are no strangers to the stress on exam day—the butterflies in the tummy, the dry mouth and perspiring palms. Under such stress the first thing that changes is our breathing.

Breathing control is relatively easy and if you can keep your breathing at a low even rate your body will relax. Try either of these two techniques.

(a) *The five-step breathing technique*
Take five completely relaxed breaths feeling your stomach moving and your stomach muscles relaxing.

Breath 1 Breathe in deeply and out again fully. For the next four breaths tense a group of muscles as you breathe in and relax them as you breathe out.
Breath 2 Feet
Breath 3 Hands and arms
Breath 4 Jaw
Breath 5 Stomach

(b) *Blowing the candle*
Imagine a candle is lit just three feet away now practice regular gentle breathing trying to make the candlelight flicker but not blowing it out.

Clasp your hands gently and breathe slowly and deeply five or six times, each time making the candle flicker.

These exercises really work. Try them and they will give you the necessary composure when you enter the exam room.

3—Reading the paper

The first minutes of the examination are crucial and, if spent constructively, will form the foundation for success. On several of the Institute's papers, 15 minutes reading time is now allowed, but in any event these first minutes of the examination should be spent in:

* assimilating the instructions
* analysing and selecting the questions

* allocating your time
* planning your answers

(a) *Checking the instructions*
Having prepared, following the guidelines.
From the last chapter you will know that the points to note are:

* how many questions are to be answered in total
* which, if any, are the compulsory questions
* how many questions are there per section
* specific instructions, e.g. 'ignore current lending restrictions'.

(b) *Reading the questions*

* Read *all* the questions carefully, but do not make your choice at this stage. In an effort to reduce their anxiety candidates often scan the questions superficially in the hope of finding their favourite topics—these first impressions may be misleading.
* Read *all* the questions for a second time, selecting the likely questions. Use a marker pen to pick out:

Key words
Imperatives
Presentational hints

These features will direct you to an answer which is *relevant* in terms of content, approach and presentation.

Key words
Key words are the words which are intended to direct the student towards the subject which forms the basis of the question.

For example, the question: 'Examine carefully the size and structure of the UK domestic banking system'.

The key words here are *size* and *structure*. It is an examination of these two characteristics of the domestic commercial banking system which is required—not a rambling essay on the subject in general.

The identification of key words will enable you to produce an answer with *relevant* content.

Imperatives
Imperatives are the words of instruction which tell the candidate the way in which the subject is to be approached.
    Examples of imperatives include:

Discuss
Define
Explain
Illustrate

Although these are common words, their use is often confused. Ensure that you are familiar with their precise meanings, in order that you can adopt a *relevant* approach. A glossary of imperatives and their meanings is provided in the appendix.
    Often a subject is to be approached in two ways, in which case you will be presented with a *double imperative,* such as:

Explain and discuss
Compare and contrast

The important point to remember is to obey *both* parts of the instructions.

Presentational hints
Questions often contain not only *key words* and *imperatives* but also *specific instructions on presentation*.

For example, 'Using four *main* headings, describe *briefly* the role played by banks in the field of international trade'. Under each heading show *concisely* the relevant services normally provided by banks. *Lengthy explanations* and *detailed examples* are not required.
    In this example there is a clear indication as to how the answer is to be presented. A concise tabular form of layout is required, rather than an essay-type presentation. Follow such instructions to produce a *relevant* form of presentation.
    Two final points on the choice of questions:

(i) Ensure that you can answer the specific question *as set*. It is essential that your answer is *relevant,* and you must, therefore, be able to address yourself to the particular requirements of the question. Do not assume you can answer the question simply because the general topic is one with which you believe you are familiar.

(ii) Do not automatically avoid *long* or *multi-part* questions. When broken down into their constituent parts, these questions can often be more straightforward than the 'one-liners'. If you do tackle questions with more than one part, make sure that you answer *all parts*.

4—Which order to answer?

Having selected your questions carefully, it is now time to consider the order in which they should be answered. There are advocates of the 'best question second' approach, who contend that during your first answer you are still nervous and that by the time you start your second question you will be ready to perform at your best. This approach may work for some students but, as a general rule, it is advisable to answer *your best question first*, because:

* it is likely to boost your confidence for the rest of the paper
* it will create a good first impression with the examiner, who after all is only human!
* it may help you to remember points on other questions which you have selected

There is one major exception to this general rule:

The compulsory question
It is a fact that very few candidates achieve a pass mark where they have not tackled the compulsory question first, and even fewer pass when they have left the question until last.

Even if the question does not correspond with your best question, *answer the compulsory question first,* because:

* it often carries the highest number of marks
* it is often the longest and most complex question
* it is psychologically beneficial to have this question 'under your belt' as soon as possible.

5—The use of time

The self-discipline of timetabling is essential throughout your studies, but nowhere is it more important than in the final stage, the examination itself. Failure to complete all questions almost always places an intolerable burden on those questions you have answered, which can be illustrated by:

The mathematics of marks
Take for example, a paper with five questions, and a pass mark of 51 per cent. If you do only three questions they must *average* 85 per cent to pass. If you do only four questions they must *average* 63.75 per cent to pass.

But if you do all five questions, they must *average only* 51 per cent.

Also with all five questions answered, if you can achieve 65 per cent on three of the questions you can still obtain a pass (assuming you have satisfied any minimum sectional requirements) by scoring only 30 per cent on the other two—and that is only 6 marks each out of a possible 20.

On a paper with *equal marks per question,* you should allow time per question, allowing a couple of minutes for proof reading at the end. At the outset write down the time you should finish each question. You should exercise strict discipline in adhering to these times. Stop writing and start the next question on a new page. More marks will be gained in the first 10 minutes of a new question, than by prolonging the previous question by the same amount of time.

On a paper with *unequal marks,* e.g. where there is a compulsory question bearing extra marks, you should apportion your time accordingly. You should be familiar with the approximate time this question takes, because you will have undertaken:

Practice under strict examination conditions

'I ran out of time' is a frequent and often convenient excuse for failure. Excuses should not be necessary for the candidate with discipline and courage.

6—Writing the answers

(a) *Points to remember*
   (i) *Create answer plans* before starting each answer.

   * Jotting down an outline covering the main points may help ensure that you do not forget something important

* This helps to produce a relevant and structured answer
* You create a good impression with the examiner, as being a more disciplined candidate.

(ii) *Be concise.* Make sure your sentences are short and to the point. No marks are awarded for waffle no matter how elegantly presented. A concise answer can often be produced by use of *tabulation,* i.e. producing the answer in a series of points.

Tabulation is actively encouraged by the Institute for most papers. Use it whenever possible:

* to save time
* to marshal your thoughts
* to avoid repetition

(iii) *Show all workings* on numerical questions and *make a rough check of your answer.* The most important part of such questions is the *method*—if you do produce the wrong answers, no marks can be awarded for method if your workings are not set out clearly.

A rough check of your answer will often indicate whether a basic error has been made in your calculations.

(b) *Points to avoid*

(i) *Repeating the question*
This is unnecessary. The question should be analysed and dissected, not repeated.

(ii) *Waffle*
Padding will not gain marks, and will antagonise the examiner —remember that answers are marked, not weighed!

(iii) *Sarcasm and slang, flattery and humour*
This creates a bad impression—why make the examiner more critical than he or she needs to be? In any case many papers contain their share of unintended humour!

(iv) *Illegibility and poor spelling*
Poor handwriting and weak spelling also create a bad impression and are unlikely to help you to gain the discretionary marks the examiner may have. Remember the obvious point—answers which cannot be read, cannot be marked.

7—Use of time at the end of the examination

Try to plan the paper so that you have a few minutes spare at the end. Do not sit back and relax, or leave the examination room, because now is the time when those extra marks can be gained, to turn a marginal paper into a pass. Use the time to:

* locate errors, particularly on numerical questions
* clarify unclear or illegible parts of your answers
* add additional relevant points

8—After the examination

Do not engage in post-mortems with colleagues, particularly when you have other parts to sit. If their answers do not agree with yours, this could adversely affect your confidence and performance in subsequent papers.

6 | Main Causes of Examination Failure

In this final chapter, we will look at the subject of examination technique from a different perspective, by considering why candidates *fail* the Institute's examinations. Regular reference will be made to the comments contained in examiners' reports, since chief examiners are more familiar than most with the causes of failure.

The same comments come up year in and year out. If students would just put into practice the techniques mentioned elsewhere in this booklet they would save themselves and the examiners much heartache.

Broadly speaking the reasons for failure are four fold.

1. Failure to appreciate what the examination is about
2. Failure to prepare adequately
3. Failure to answer the question as set
4. Failure to complete the paper

This short list is not intended to be exhaustive, nor should it be thought that the reasons are mutually exclusive.

For example, both points 3 and 4 are often a direct result of 2, whilst 1 is more than likely to lead to 2, 3 and 4. However, this quartet of 'failures' emerges from examiners' reports with such predictable regularity, that re-emphasis is worthwhile in an effort to reinforce the chief examiner's regular pleadings.

1—Failure to appreciate what the examination is about

The Institute's examinations are not meant to be tests of knowledge alone. They are intended to ensure that students:

* know the appropriate content
* can interrelate the components of knowledge
* can put their knowledge (and their answers) into the wider picture.

Increasingly, the Institute's examinations are concerned with the *application* of knowledge to practical situations, and cannot be passed merely by the use of good memory. Hence a broad-based knowledge of the subject is essential.

Students who concentrate on learning and then regurgitating facts alone are virtually doomed to failure. However, students who understand how to use these facts to solve wider problems enhance their chances of passing tremendously.

"The examination should not be a test of memory but of understanding, and a candidate who explains what he says, and is capable of sensible elaboration of principle, should score more highly than a person who simply presents the correct conclusions (as he sees it)."

(LAW RELATING TO BANKING)

"The right approach involves an understanding of basic principles of law, and the ability to apply those principles to a set of facts, when appropriate."

(LAW RELATING TO BANKING)

"Candidates should be reminded that economics is not a 'memory' subject: it is a way of thinking, of analysing and commenting on problems and situations which do exist in the business of banking."

(ECONOMICS AND THE BANKS' ROLE IN THE ECONOMY)

2—Failure to prepare adequately

The whole of the study year is a preparation for the examination and students should remember that *failure to prepare is preparation for failure*. Preparation is not just going to evening classes or studying in your room; it is about making sure that:

* the study year is planned (you cover the syllabus)

* each study period is organised

* revision is organised

"Examination results would have shown a much higher pass rate if candidates had prepared themselves properly."

(FINANCE OF INTERNATIONAL TRADE)

(i) *Insufficient work*

Although study and examination techniques are important in ensuring that students get the best out of themselves, they cannot by themselves get a student through the exam successfully. It is only where technique is added to regular and dedicated studying that success can be virtually guaranteed.

"Candidates do not fail because of difficult examination papers or unduly hard marking, but because they simply have not done sufficient work and do not know enough."

(LAW RELATING TO BANKING)

Candidates for the Institute's exams cannot hope to achieve success without a considerable amount of hard work and application. Yet all too often it appears that students are willing to 'have a go', particularly for the Autumn papers, when they are wholly unprepared. This is an unprofessional approach and merely serves to give candidates a convenient excuse for failure.

"The (Autumn) examinations should not be treated as an occasion just to 'have a go'. A proper programme of work and study is essential. The examiner was left wondering how many students had really buckled down to what was necessary."

(PRACTICE OF BANKING 1)

(ii) *Inadequate coverage of the syllabus*

The Institute publishes a syllabus for every subject; students should use them to plan their study year. Many students arrive at the examination without having covered enough topics or have not covered them in sufficient depth. Even though there is a choice in the examination, students should use the syllabus to ensure that they cover all the necessary subject matter. Some students prepare to fail by not planning their study year in September.

"In both sections of the paper there was a question which was avoided by many candidates presumably because they had not studied the whole syllabus. It is essential that candidates cover the whole of the syllabus and can also apply their technical knowledge to the practical situation which is met in branch banking when such areas are encountered."

(PRACTICE OF BANKING 1)

Remember it is important to have the latest syllabus so that you can spot any new topics which have appeared. It is often the case that new items will form the basis of questions in the following examination.

Many candidates endeavour to take a short-cut in their preparation by concentrating on those subjects which they believe are due to come up. All too often, however, the range of topics selected is so narrow that if their 'banker' questions do not appear, the paper cannot be completed in any meaningful sense.

(iii) *Inadequate depth of knowledge*

After every examination most examiners encounter several blank answer books. Apart from the rare occasion where a candidate is completely immobilised by examination nerves, this indicates a total lack of preparation.

"It is surprising to find that there are candidates at this level who cannot get beyond writing their name and address on the script cover."

(PRACTICE OF BANKING 2)

Fortunately, this is not typical, but what is typical is that candidates often grasp the bones of a question but fail, because of inadequate preparation, to put sufficient flesh on it.

"Many candidates suffered from an approach which was far too superficial."

(INVESTMENT)

"Very many candidates showed their lack of proper preparation by the superficiality and irrelevance of much of their answers."

(INVESTMENT)

Part of the problem is that candidates are too restrictive in the breadth of their studies and believe that their college courses, or their one standard textbook, will provide sufficient material for success. The following comments are typical.

"Candidates do not read extensively enough"
(NATURE OF MANAGEMENT)

"It is important that candidates should be sufficiently interested in the subject to read through, at least once, the textbooks suggested as recommended reading and further reading."
(INVESTMENT)

(iv) *Failure to keep up-to-date*
We emphasised the importance of keeping up-to-date in the second chapter when it was noted that the banking industry was subject to constant change. It is vital therefore, that you should keep abreast of recent developments in your subjects. All too often, however, the Chief Examiner's exhortations to keep up-to-date fall on deaf ears.

". . . two of the questions covered aspects which have only recently been recognised as significant. Each of them has been the subject of comment in the *Banking World* and bank circulars—if candidates had only attempted to keep up-to-date they would surely have had no problems."
(PRACTICE OF BANKING 2)

(v) *Misconceptions*
The superficial approach to preparation often results in a lack of understanding, which manifests itself in a variety of 'howlers' such as:

"The partnership overdraft should be secured by the partners' personal guarantees."

"Eurocurrency is money purchased to go on holiday to Europe."

"Forward foreign exchange rates are determined by the forecasts of dealers."

Sadly these examples are all too common. The Institute's examinations are intended to prepare bankers for the real world and examiners cannot consider candidates as being qualified in their subjects when they exhibit such basic misconceptions.

"Many candidates...did not possess a proper grasp of the subject. Passing is seen as an end in itself rather than the means by which staff who are striving to equip themselves for positions they may be called upon to fill, demonstrate that they are masters of their subject."

(FINANCE OF INTERNATIONAL TRADE)

3—Failure to answer the question

If an analysis is made of reasons for failure amongst capable students, an outstanding feature is that students manage to answer one question badly. This failure is often due to either selecting the wrong question or not leaving enough time to answer the last question (see section 4).

"What is required is the ability to put together five decent answers instead of, all too frequently, only a couple, with the remainder being disastrous."

(LAW RELATING TO BANKING)

(i) *Selecting the wrong question*

As was mentioned earlier, students should read the questions carefully looking for those words which reduce the content to an amount that can be handled in 30 minutes, and looking out for the order of words which tell you what to do with the material. Unless students spot these key words (and therefore deal with the right subject matter), then use the material as instructed (through the order words), they will not be able to answer the question that is set correctly.

"...many ignored the word 'list' and made a verbose meal of the answer ..."

(INVESTMENT)

"Although the question stated 'consider the *liability,* of the other two partners', numerous answers went way off the mark by dealing with the rights of the other partners."

(LAW RELATING TO BANKING)

You must select only those questions that you can actually answer.

(ii) *Failure to read the question properly*

It is apparent that many candidates approach the important task of reading the question paper in a perfunctory and haphazard manner, despite the inclusion of 15 minutes reading time on many papers.

"Candidates are now given an additional 15 minutes to read through the question paper prior to the examination. Nevertheless, there was plenty of evidence that students continue to pay insufficient care and attention to this task."

(ACCOUNTANCY)

A superficial and hurried reading of the question may often be misleading. As a result:

"Many candidates give the answer to the question they wished they had been asked."

(NATURE OF MANAGEMENT)

After an initial quick reading of the questions many candidates plunge into the answers without further thought, ignoring those vital words in a question which should lead students towards a relevant answer.

"Candidates should go through each of the questions selected underlining the key words. These key words should tell the candidate what it is that the examiner requires—which is why the examiner put them in the question."

(MONETARY ECONOMICS)

(iii) *Spotting questions*

The advice to read all the questions before making a choice is partly an attempt to stop students from trying to spot questions.

Spotting questions leads to two possible problems, firstly, the subject comes up, secondly, it does not. If the subject area is on the paper, the problem with 'spotting' is that students see the subject area and then ignore the question and answer as if the question read "...write all you know about...".

Unless the specific question set can be answered, question 'spotting' can lead to disaster. If, on the other hand, the 'spotted' areas do not appear, panic may strike and failure may result.

"Candidates had come prepared to write all they knew on a subject, and hardly bothered to read the question or to apply their material to the facts given."

(LAW RELATING TO BANKING)

"Once again, one sees a number of candidates who attempt to 'question spot' and answer a question which may have been asked some time ago, instead of the one which is actually asked."

(FINANCE OF INTERNATIONAL TRADE)

(iv) *Waffle*

Nothing is more certain to guarantee poor marks than the production of reams of irrelevant material, often completely at a tangent to the question in hand.

"The blunderbuss approach usually suggests that the candidate has failed to identify the basic point of the question and is simply hoping that a few stray shots will hit the target."

(PRACTICE OF BANKING 2)

Whether it is because the thrust of the question is imperfectly understood, misread, or simply ignored, many candidates seem determined to record all the information which might be remotely connected with the subject in hand. Marks will only be awarded for those points which are relevant to the questions posed.

"Many candidates did not read the question carefully enough and included waffle."

(INVESTMENT)

"The majority of candidates write long-winded answers running to many pages despite the continuous plea from the examiner for brevity."

(FINANCE OF INTERNATIONAL TRADE)

(v) *Poor presentation*
Students who present their answers neatly and legibly are more likely to score high marks. Remember, if an examiner cannot read them he cannot mark them.

"There are numerous examples of scripts in which the student has apparently taken little pride."

(BUSINESS OF BANKING)

4—Failure to complete the paper

Not completing the paper is the second reason why students do the one poor answer that leads to failure. Believe it or not, examiners like to pass candidates, and it is disappointing to see failures, not because they were badly prepared, or because their answers were irrelevant, but because they had not completed the paper due to lack of time.

"There is some evidence that poor performance in one question is caused by poor rationing of the available time rather than by lack of knowledge. For example, it is asking for trouble to write 12½ pages on one question, leaving time for only half-a-dozen lines on the last question attempted."

(PRACTICE OF BANKING 2)

Avoid this happening by *organising yourself;* examiners do not expect students to be writing for three hours. Students should set aside time to plan answers and to read them through at the end of the examination. The time to be spent on each question should be worked out before the student goes into the examination room and when the allocated time is ended the student should stop and move on to the next question. This simple discipline always ensures that there is enough time for the last question.

Writing out the question is a common and time wasting habit. There is no need to write the question out in full or in part—the examiner already knows what it is—he set the paper and he has a copy anyway. All students need to do is to number the question correctly, the examiner will do the rest.

"There is still a tendency by far too many students to write out the question, albeit in précis form. This bad practice meant that, in a few cases, candidates were unable to complete their last answer adequately."

(PRACTICE OF BANKING 1)

"Students wasted time writing out the question in their answer book rather than using the time to write the answer."

(BUSINESS OF BANKING)

Not writing too much has already been mentioned before but it is worth restating that examiners are only expecting around 25 to 30 minutes to be spent on actually writing out the answer. Writing page after page is usually a sign of not answering the specific question or that there is a lot of 'waffling going on'.

There should be no excuses for running out of time, since many of the questions in the Institute's papers specifically call for brief, concise answers which could be completed well within the time allowed.

"When the examiner clearly states that brief notes or tabulation are required, candidates will not gain any credit for long, rambling answers."

(FINANCE OF INTERNATIONAL TRADE)

The examiners' reports abound in pleas for answers to be presented in a tabular form when appropriate, yet too few candidates appear to have the courage to respond to these requests.

"Overall, last year's plea by the examiner for concise, tabulated and pre-planned answers appeared to have been ignored to a large extent, and the plea is reiterated in the hope that it will be heeded."

(PRACTICE OF BANKING 2)

To conclude, the following quote from a Chief Examiner summarises the main causes of examination failure (and also shows the frustration felt by the examiner). *Please help the examiner to help you by avoiding these mistakes in future examinations.*

"At the risk of flogging a dead horse, one has to say that the age-old problems manifested themselves yet again:

(a)   Not reading the question and not answering it as set;
(b)   Not answering five questions;
(c)   Too much time spent on the first question and (seemingly) thereby running out of time;
(d)   *Too* theoretical an approach. Little attempt to relate to the type of business, and the specific problem being examined;
(e)   Illegibility."

(PRACTICE OF BANKING 2)

AN APPENDIX OF IMPERATIVES

Advise   Present recommendations to

Appraise   Estimate the importance or value of

Amplify   Expand or enlarge upon (a statement or quotation)

Analyse   Examine minutely the individual constituent parts of a theory or policy and their interrelationship

Assess   Estimate the value or importance of a theory or policy

Clarify   Present clearly by explaining complications

Comment   Make remarks based upon evidence

Compare   Look for similarities and differences between

Consider   Weigh the merits of

Contrast   Place in opposition to bring out difference

Criticize   Present the faults in a theory or policy or opinion

Define   Give the precise meaning of

Demonstrate   Logically prove the truth of

Describe   Present the details and characteristics of

Discuss   Examine by argument giving the pros and cons

Distinguish   Point to the differences between

Enumerate   Specify items giving their numbers

Evaluate   Place a value on a theory, policy or opinion in the light of an appraisal based on selected criteria

Examine	Investigate in detail a theory or statement or proposition
Explain	Set out in detail the meaning of
Illustrate	Make clear by specific examples and/or use a chart diagram, graph or figure to explain and clarify
Justify	Present adequate grounds for
List	Give a catalogue of
Outline	Show the essential parts of, or the main features, or the general principles. Overall structure and relationships are required, *not* minor details
Prove	Test the accuracy of
Reconcile	Make compatible or harmonise apparently conflicting statements or theories
Relate	Show connections between separate points or narrate
Review	Present a survey or possibly a retrospective survey calling for a critical analysis
State	Express fully or clearly
Summarize	Present a brief account of the essential points dispensing with examples and details
Trace	Follow the development of a theory

North London College of Accountancy

145 Stamford Hill, London N16 5LG
Tel: 01-809 5559

SCHOOL OF BANKING

A quick route to your

ACIB

Both BANKING CERTIFICATE & DIPLOMA

Fees: £150.00 per subject
Intakes: January/July each year
Featuring:
(1) Small classes (15 Students)
(2) Well furnished modern classrooms
(3) Professionally qualified lecturers

**COURSES COMPLY WITH HOME OFFICER
REQUIREMENT FOR FOREIGN STUDENTS.** College Accommodation Available.

CITY BUSINESS COLLEGE

specialist college for

BANKING
BUSINESS STUDIES
D.M.S. M.B.A.

**BANKING CERTIFICATE PRELIMINARY SECTION
COURSES STARTING JULY, SEPTEMBER & JANUARY**

BANKING FOUNDATION
INTERNAL EXAMINATION WITHIN 6 MONTHS
F/TIME COURSES COMMENCING JULY, SEPTEMBER & JANUARY
BANKING STAGE 2 INTERNATIONAL BANKING DIPLOMA
F/TIME COURSES - start OCTOBER & JULY
12 WEEK F/TIME REVISION COURSES
STARTING JANUARY & AUGUST
ALSO PART TIME & DAY RELEASE

EXPERT TUITION BY PROFESSIONAL STAFF

CONTACT: THE REGISTRAR, C.B.C.,
178 GOSWELL ROAD, LONDON, EC1
01-251 6473/01-251 0427

Write to or Telephone: 0227-762600

BANKERS BOOKS LIMITED
THE CHARTERED INSTITUTE OF BANKERS
EMMANUEL HOUSE
4-9 BURGATE LANE
CANTERBURY
KENT CT1 2XJ

or

Visit Reception

THE CHARTERED INSTITUTE OF BANKERS
10 LOMBARD STREET
LONDON EC3V 9AS
TEL: 01 623 3531
FAX: 01 283 1510

or

Visit Bookshop

BANKERS BOOKS LIMITED
17 ST. SWITHIN'S LANE
LONDON EC4N 8AL
TEL: 01 929 4306
FAX: 01 929 4301

ACCESS AND VISA CARDS ACCEPTED